MINDFULNESS

FOR

BEGINNERS

Make the Most Out of Your Life

By Martin Brandt

Table of Contents

What Is Mindulness

Congratulations! You have just decided to better your life by downloading this book. *Mindfulness for Beginners: Make the Most Out of Your Life* will teach you everything you need to know about Mindfulness and the practices that it encompasses.

What is Mindfulness? It is the essential human capacity to be totally present, aware of what we are doing as well as where we are. Mindfulness is something that everyone possesses. However, it is something that requires practice to nurture the abilities.

In this book, you will learn all the techniques needed to find your mindfulness and how to practice it daily as well as the fundamentals of why this practice can help you to manage stress, relationships, work and create an overall better you.

In this book, we will discuss first what stress is, how it affects your mind and body, and how to manage it. We will then go through the first steps of Mindfulness and what is required as you begin training your mind. You will learn what your narrative is, how to be non-judgmental, how to curb greed, liberate yourself from suffering, and how to rid yourself of the delusions of self-fulfilling prophecies.

Lastly, after we have discussed how to allow your mind to start processing all of that clutter, we will learn techniques you can use to practice mindfulness daily. Techniques for mindfulness in breathing, mindfulness in eating, mindfulness in emotions and thought, and mindfulness of sounds. All this awaits you, so let's begin.

Chapter 1: Help! I'm So Stressed!

In today's modern world of nonstop, go-go-go attitudes, where there are deadlines to be made, a to-do list that is getting out of hand, raising kids, paying bills, you name it, it's very easy to become stressed out. Does this sound familiar? Everyone gets stressed, everyone reaches their limit. It is a normal process, especially in modern society. But it is not so much the stress that is the issue, it is how you deal with it. Let us consider what stress is, and how we can deal with it.

Stress is typically a physical response the body takes when it believes it is under attack. The body takes what is known as the "fight or flight" mode, which then makes it release certain hormones called norepinephrine, adrenaline, and cortisol, which are what makes your body prepared for action. These hormones get pumped into through your bloodstream to be deposited in places like your muscles so you can react quickly, your brain to be able to make quick decisions, and they also can other functions of the body to stop altogether, such as digestion so that all awareness is focused on the act of fight or flight. When you are placed in a dangerous situation, or any situation where the flight or flight mode may be needed, it is considered to be a healthy form of stress on the body, one which we are born with. This form of stress has been within the human being for thousands of years, and used to the advantages of ancient civilizations, such as the caveman who needed this to avoid being eaten or to focus on hunting that mammoth, Without this form of stress, we may not survive those moments where quick action is needed, such as avoiding a car accident.

However, when our bodies enter a constant state of stress, blood flow changes and gets diverted from the brain for that fight or flight mode, and then that lowers the brain's ability to function properly. This can inhibit your ability to function normally. This can become harmful to your health if the body stays in that state for extended amounts of time. The cortisol hormone has been known to decrease libido and increase glucose and blood pressure levels when there is too much of it in the body.

The fight or flight reaction can affect your body in three separate ways when it is activated, and depending on which type of person you are, each way can have major outcomes in your life.

Fight mode: When your body enters into a stressed fight mode state, your mood changes, causing you to become aggressive or agitated toward others. This is part of the natural "fight" process of stress reactions. However, in the day to day life, this can end up affecting relationships and character negatively.

Flight mode: For others, fight may not be your initial reaction. You may be the type that avoids your stressors. You do this by removing yourself from the situation instead of facing it. This is your flight mode kicking in. In a natural disaster situation that flight mode is helpful, but in everyday life? Your natural instinct actually may lead to the stressful situation getting bigger, which then increases your stress levels as you realize the issue is not going to go away by avoiding it.

Freeze mode: This is a reaction that many do not realize is part of the "fight or flight" response. Instead of getting pumped with adrenaline to fight off the attack, or the quick decision to run, some people freeze when they are under stress. This, needless to say, does not help your stressor either, as you are unable to do anything about it.

Why is it so important to manage stress? Because as we have seen, living with constant high levels of stress puts your well-being in danger. Stress can destroy your emotional state of mind and your physical health. When you are stressed, your ability to think clearly is even impaired, and therefore you cannot take pleasure in your life. By managing your stress, you will be helping yourself to end the grasp it has on your life. This will help you to become a healthier, more useful, and more contented you. By practicing some stress management routines, your life will become more stable, with time for work, associations, recreation, and fun. And with practice, the ability to stand up to stress and challenges head-on.

Stress management takes practice, and every technique does not always work for everyone. Through trial and error, you can find the right tools for you to relieve stress. Here are a few tips on how to start ridding yourself of the stress in your life.

Identify the source

The first step is to obviously figure out what it is that is causing the stress. For some, this may be very easy to figure out because they are experiencing major life stressors such as job change, divorce, health issues, money issues, etc., chronic stress can be a little tougher to pinpoint. We tend to overlook our own feelings, thoughts, and actions, and thus not realize how much they may be affecting your stress levels. Example: you are constantly worried about deadlines, and you think the deadline is the issue when in reality, it might be your tendency to procrastinate rather than the demands of the job.

Ask yourself these questions while you are trying to self-examine yourself and find your source of stress: Do you try to reason that your stress is temporary, as in, "I have so much going on right now..."? Is stress defined by you as just a normal part of work or home life? Is it easy to blame others or events for your stress? Unless you can accept responsibility for your own actions in your levels of stress, it will remain outside of your power to manage it.

One tip some have tried is to start what is called a stress journal. This can help you figure out any regular stressors and how you deal with them. Every time you start to feel stressed, write it down in your journal. As you start keeping a log, you may notice some patterns and common issues. When you start to feel stressed some good things to write about in your entry are: what is causing your stress at the moment, and if you are not sure throw a guess or two in there; how you are feeling, emotionally and physically; how you are responding to the stressor; and what did you do to make yourself feel better.

Practice what is known as the 4 A's of stress management

Stress can be predictable or unpredictable. For the predictable stressors, like a meeting with your boss, the daily commute, or dealing with family, it is possible for you to change your situation or your reactions. To do this, you can follow the 4 A's: Avoid, Alter, Adapt, Accept.

Avoid: You can avoid unnecessary stress.

- Learn to say "no." Learn your limits and stick to them so you can avoid taking on too much.

- Stay away from people that stress you out. This can be a tough one, especially if they are family, but if there is someone that regularly causes you stress, limit your association or end the relationship completely.

- Control what is around you: If traffic bothers you, try an alternate route that has less traffic, even if it may make the commute longer, if the news bothers you, turn the channel or turn off the TV, or if shopping is something you hate, ask someone else to help or shop online. Remove the issues around you that cause stress.

- Simplify your to-do list: Take a look at your schedule and daily tasks. Do you have too much on your plate? Simplify it. Move less important things to the bottom of the list, or even better, get rid of them completely.

Alter your situation: Learn to find ways to think differently

- Start talking about your feelings, do not hold them inside. If there is something that is bothering you, say it. If left to sit in your mind, it can fester, and that can lead to all sorts of stress and negative emotions.

- Compromise: If you think someone else's behavior is the reason for your stress, and you ask them to change, you should be willing to change yourself. Finding middle ground is always healthier and will eliminate stress

- Balance your schedule: Burnout, the dreaded word of the working class. Try to find some downtime, put family life, social pursuits and even alone time as a priority to help balance your work and personal life.

Adapt to what stresses you: If you can't fix the stressor then change how you deal with it

- Rethink problems: View a stressful situation in a more positive light.

- The bigger picture: Look at the stressful situation and ask yourself, how important is it really? Will it matter in a week? A month? A year? If you can answer no, then ignore it and focus on something more important

- Change your standards: This one can be tough for some people. Perfectionism is a huge source of stress that is completely avoidable. Stop setting your standards so high so that you can actually meet some goals and expectations.

Exercise

Exercise is one the best cures for stress. But when you are stressed it usually is the last thing you feel like doing. When you are stressed you can be in physical pain, tight shoulders, stiff neck, jaw muscles ache, migraines. Sound familiar? Of course, exercise does not sound fun. However, it is actually crucial to relieving that tension. Exercise makes your body release endorphins, and they make you feel good. Exercise can also help distract you from your daily stressors. The general recommendation is 30 minutes or more of exercise daily, you do not have to be an athlete or gym-o-holic who gets up at 4 am to go run 10 miles, any form of physical activity is beneficial, especially if you are just starting out. The point is to get up and get moving.

Simple activities to start with:

- Play a movement-based video game with your kids, like tennis or dancing

- Park a little farther away from the store or your office

- Walk the dog

- Good music to dance to

- Try walking or bicycling to work or the store

- Take the stairs instead of the elevator

- Find someone else who wants to exercise and make it a fun partnership

Schedule some time for relaxation

So far we have discussed ways to take charge and keep a positive attitude, but getting downtime is also crucial to stress management. Living in the nonstop world we do, it can be easy to forget to take care of yourself and your needs. Making that time for relaxation will help you find that happy place where you will be able to take on life's stressors a little better.

- Set your leisure time: You should try for this daily. This is the chance to unplug and take a break from all your obligations, so do not let other responsibilities get in the way.

- What do you enjoy? Do it every day. Your resting activities should be something you actually like doing, even if it is just staring out at the stars at night, make sure that is what you find the time to do.

- Laugh at yourself: Laughter is very therapeutic, and a sense of humor can help fight stress

Talk to someone

When you are stressed, thoughts and feelings become all one big jumble inside you. Talking it out can help to alleviate some of those bothersome feelings.

- Stress can cloud your ability to think clearly, so talking things out can be very helpful

- A trusted friend or your spouse can lend an ear, and may even have some helpful answers for you.

- Sometimes just saying what is bothering out loud can help relieve the stress, because as you say it, you may just realize how silly that matter is.

- Don't keep things bottled up if there is a repetitive thought of feelings that just won't go away, talk to someone. It can help relieve a lot of stress.

Time Management

When you stretch yourself too thin, you can get stressed because it is hard to stay on top of things, and you are unable to stay calm and focused. When you overbook yourself, you also are unable to get the time you need to feel better, such as your leisure time and a good night's sleep.

- Don't over commit yourself. Don't schedule things back to back or fit it all into one day. It never works and will cause more stress than if you had done it on separate days.

- Prioritize: Take a look at what to do list and pick the ones that must get done, and put the rest in order of importance.

- Let others help: It is ok to ask for help and let others assist you. Trying to do everything yourself whether it is at home or at work can be a huge cause of stress. Stop trying to control it all and give tasks to others.

Have a healthy lifestyle

Besides exercise, there are other things you can do for yourself to be healthy and help minimize your stress levels.

- Eat healthier: Be aware of what you eat. Eat a good breakfast so that you can focus throughout the day, and eat regular balanced meals.

- Limit caffeine and sugar: Caffeine is an upper, and sugar can give you a nice boost of energy as well, however, once those highs wear off, it can cause that crashing sensation we all hate so much. By limiting the amounts you eat, you won't get those crashes and will feel better

- Limit alcohol: When you are stressed it is easy to want to turn to alcohol and natural remedy to help you relax and not feel so edgy. However, this is only a temporary relief, and it only serves to hide your real issues.

- Sleep: A good night's sleep is crucial to maintaining a healthy lifestyle but also to reduce stress. Your body needs that time to recharge and reset for the next day

Dealing with stress is never easy, and there is never one easy way to rid yourself of it. Life still has to go on each day, and with it will bring its own new doses of stress. But with practice and maintaining some healthy habits, you can manage your stress levels. You might even eliminate some all together! There are other techniques for managing stress as well, as well as a whole mindset that you can achieve with practice. It is called Mindfulness. What is it? The next chapter will discuss what Mindfulness is as well as how you can start to practice it.

Chapter 2: How to Enter a Beginners Mindset

In the previous chapter we learned about stress, how it can be caused and the effect it can have on you mentally and physically. We even discussed several ways on how to manage your stress levels and maintain a healthier lifestyle. But what about your mind as a whole? How can you achieve that inner Zen that so many seem to have found? You can start with learning about Mindfulness.

In Zen Buddhism, there is a concept called *shoshin*, which translated means "beginner's mind." Shoshin is based on the premise that you can let go of your preconceived ideas and have an attitude of openness to new concepts.

With the practice of Mindfulness gaining popularity among not only those who practice meditation but also among the psychotherapy community, it is easy to learn more about the practice and how to progress. Some of the benefits you can learn from the practice of mindfulness are learning self-control, tolerance, enhanced flexibility of mind, equanimity, and objectivity.

So what is Mindfulness and its practices? Mindfulness is the ability to be present and fully aware of what you are doing and where you are, while not being overwhelmed or overly reactive by what is going on around you. This means that your mind is completely aware of what is happening, what you are doing, and the space that you move through. Mindfulness helps you to respond reflectively to a situation rather than reacting to them because of habits you have been conditioned to. Mindfulness uses the experiences of the moment, including sounds, sensations in the body, smells, tastes, and breathing, as a way to anchor nonjudgmental attention, stabilizing your way of relating to your inner and outer experiences.

Mindfulness is not special. It is not added. The power to be in the present is already born within us. You just need to learn how to harness it. There are simple practices one can learn that have been scientifically proven to benefit yourself, those you love, friends, and coworkers. There is no need to change for mindfulness either. When an answer to a problem presents itself in the form of changing yourself, it typically fails. Change is hard. Mindfulness acknowledges this and brings out the best of who you are as a person.

Meditation is not something that is only in your head. It does not mean dwelling on your thoughts either. Meditation is based on your body. It requires you taking the time to listen to where you are and what you are doing, which generally starts with being aware of your body. This act can be very calming as you get in tune with your body's rhythms.

Mindfulness and Awareness

Mindfulness and Awareness go hand in hand. Mindfulness requires you to relate to your current situation definitely, directly, and precisely. The way you deal with irritating or frustrating situations usually involves emotions like aggression, restlessness, passion, and ignorance. These feelings are normal in today's world. They do not need to be shunned, you can consider them more like fits, such as a toddler would have, only this is your body reacting. You have been conditioned to react these ways, however, depending on your situation, they could be the precise reaction needed for that moment's frustrations. Being in a mindful state is just another way to clearly show what is there in front of you. This means that you are only aware of your active mind, which can be involved in several perceptions. The mind does not deal with the past or the future, it simply lives in the now. It is necessary when beginning to be aware of these dual perceptions because it helps you to refrain from making quick judgments.

Awareness, however, is being able to see the breakthrough of mindfulness. Through awareness, you can leave what is in your mind be, instead of tossing it away like yesterdays garbage. Mindfulness has its own location and space within the brain. Because of this awareness, you can take one more step to being able not to choose in a situation, or being "choiceless." This simply means that you react without judging, you recognize that it is what it is. Recognizing, or "recognition," the outcomes mindfulness can give you, such as recognizing passions, aggressions, frustrations, sadness, happiness, and joys, is also a large part of awareness. Another way of explaining this is by asking yourself "What should I do with this feeling I am experiencing right now?" or "What can I do next about this?" Having awareness then helps us to see that we do not necessarily need to do anything really, but can leave it to be in its own place within your mind.

Consider this example: You notice a beautiful flower while on a hike. Do you pick it and take it home with you? Or do you allow the flower to stay there in its natural environment? Awareness tells you to leave the flower alone because it is where it is meant to be. This means that awareness is the ability to be willing to not hang on to discoveries made by being mindful. Mindfulness is an act of being able to recognize that things are what they are. Because of this, mindfulness and awareness work together as a way to help you find acceptance in situations as they arise.

The practice of meditation is how you can diffuse yourself of stress. The amount of meditation you do often depend on the amount of stress that you are under. There are several ways to begin meditation, and a lot of it has to do with your physical locations, how you sit, breathe, and the environment around you. We will go into meditation and some exercises in depth in a later chapter, however, here are a few specific things you can do now to alleviate some of the anxieties and stress you may be experiencing, or encounter in the future.

Beginning Your Meditation

How you sit can play a large part in the process of meditation. Your posture too is important when you meditate. Just sitting quietly can be a wonderful way to relax, if even for a moment, before going back to your crazy routine.

This next exercise is a quick, easy way to practice meditation wherever you are. Find a seat that is comfortable for you depending on your physical needs and location. This could be a chair, the floor, or a bench. But it should be solid. Be aware of where your legs are at. If on the floor, cross them. If in a chair or bench, have both feet touching the ground. Keep your back and upper body straight, allowing the natural curve of your spine to remain. Keep your arms to the side of your body, placing hands on top of your legs.

Next, let you gaze drop and allow your head to tilt forward just a little. Closing your eyes is often practiced, but it is not necessary. Now that you have found the proper stance for meditation, stay there a few moments. Relax and allow yourself to just focus on you at that moment. Once you have found that calmness that comes from focusing inward, you can return to your day. If you begin to feel the pains of stress again, repeat the whole thing.

This is a quick a simple way of practicing mindfulness daily, and easy for the beginner. This is all that it is, combined with some breathing techniques that we will discuss in a moment. Remembering to do this several times a day, or when you feel your blood pressure start to rise because the stress is getting to you is the hard part. As you continue to practice this, you will notice that your results will gradually grow.

Remember from the previous chapter, that stress triggers a specific response within our bodies, bringing out the primitive nature of the brain, that fight or flight response. Only after you have dealt with the current trigger will your body return to its normal state. You can get back to your normal state by practicing the mindfulness techniques at that moment, and reduce them altogether by frequent practicing.

Good times to practice these meditations are throughout your day, simply by shifting your mind away from the moment and taking a few deep breaths, or just a brief pause. Sometimes you may want to consider taking these moments could include:

- When you wake up in the morning or before bed

- Going to the bathroom

- While waiting for your computer to load

- Before answering the phone or replying to a text message

- Before and after meetings

- And especially before speaking during a stressful conversation

The next step is to not only continue to practice these quick moments of mindfulness and awareness but adding breathing to the equation. As with all types of fitness, mental fitness comes with training. So practice daily, and soon you will see the benefits begin to take hold.

Here is a simple 5-minute breathing technique you can incorporate into a mindful state of meditation. This can be done daily, or multiple times a day.

- Place yourself in a comfortable position, either practicing the sitting technique discussed earlier or laying down.

- Close your eyes if you choose. If not, allow your gaze to become unfocused, not fixating on an object.

- Turn your thoughts inward to your present moment by paying attention to what you are feeling physically. You can do this by checking your body from head to toe. Tell yourself to let any tension located in your body to go away.

- Once you have let all tension release, focus on how you are breathing. Notice your breath going in and out. Next, when you breathe, pay attention to your chest as it rises and falls. Then focus on your stomach as it rises and falls with each breath.

- Choose a vantage point to focus on, then pay attention to the breaths as they come and go. Make sure to follow the breath from start to finish, fully inhaling naturally and exhaling naturally, some may be short, long, deep, or shallow.

- If your mind wanders while focusing on each breath, which is very common, pay attention to where it wanders off to, then bring yourself back to the task at hand of felling how you are breathing and each breath going in and out.

- It is natural for the mind to wander during these sessions. Do not let this discourage you. All you need to do is to catch yourself and gently bring yourself back to the breathing exercise.

- Last, do this daily, at least for one week. At the end of the week see how you are feeling about allowing yourself time to be within yourself and allowing your body the ability to detach and therefore de-clutter.

By practicing mindful breathing, you are strengthening a muscle that helps you live in the present. The more you practice, the more you will discover how easy it will be to stay in the present, instead of getting trapped into the past or some daydream about the future. Living in the now will help you to feel more at peace and with more clarity, thus helping you to deal with difficult circumstances. Mindfulness is not a reason to tune out the world, but it is about tuning in, with more compassion and open awareness. As you being to relate to life from this vantage point, you will discover a whole new world of opportunities.

- A few things to remember about having a Beginner's Mind:

- Take one step at a time

- If you fall several times, get up several more times

- Do not pre-judge. Instead, think of it as I do not know mine

- Do not live with an "I should have" attitude

- Do not make experiences negative, instead use experience, keeping an open mind which will allow you to apply mindfulness to a new circumstance.

- Stop being the expert.

- Forget common sense

- Do not let fear of failure guide you

- Focus on the questions and not the answers.

As you develop your Beginner's mind, you learn to become much more open to new possibilities and more creative. You will forge new friendships with others as they begin to notice your interest in them and your appreciation for their ideas and thoughts on things. This is what Beginner's Mind is all about. We have covered the basis of Beginner's Mind and some basic meditation and breathing techniques to help start your journey down this path. Let us now consider how Beginner's Mind can help you in other aspects of your life, such as how to be non-judgmental, how to deal with greed, delusions, acceptance and letting go.

Chapter 3: Mindfulness-Based Stress Reduction: How to Not Take Our Thoughts Personally

Questioning Our Narrative

Your narrative is the story of your life. It is all the hurts, successes, failures, and accomplishments that you have accumulated over the course of your life. When you feel unworthy it feels like you are flawed and then must hide all your faults from everyone, or else you fear you may be shunned. However, concealing flaws, pretending, and withholding faults from others will make you begin to feel like an outcast, which then can make you believe that you truly are flawed. This cycle of self-doubting and self-judgments can leave you feeling like you are not complete. By practicing mindfulness and self-compassion, you can see the pains within your own narrative. This will help you to overcome the thinking that your negative story defines who you are. *It is not who you are.*

The stories we tell, predominantly the ones do not know are in the back of our psyche, can strongly form who we are, and from there the choices that we make. Becoming acquainted with our inner stories and how they influence how we communicate with others is a characteristic of becoming self-aware, and a large foundation of mindfulness. But it can be complicated to separate ourselves from the stories that make up our being unless we are aware of them, and from there try to understand where they began.

Each one of us can be a storyteller, it is a natural way of organizing your worlds. Through this process, the brain can categorize those memories as a way to use in the future to help calculate events, relationships, and experiences. Four millennia all cultures have used stories as a way to explain everything for how they hunted to wisdom, and pass on their traditions

The next opportunity you get when you are stopped at traffic or waiting in line at the supermarket, consider what your mind is doing. You may be surprised to find yourself recounting a story. It may be plans for the weekend, a recent article you read, or recounting a conversation you had recently that did not end well. No matter what it is, this is a story, all adding to your life's overall narrative.

How do your stories begin? It all starts at an early age. As young children, we all test the world around us in an attempt to learn what things are, and what the outcomes will be. They even tend to have exaggerated long narratives when they play because they are trying to see what fits and what does not. As an adult, you do the same thing. How it differs is that it is all in your head, which then determines our behavior and how we react to situations.

Most of the basic narratives that are created about your identity are shaped by how you were raised, what your parents perceived, and your significant others. As you receive consistent feedback, the more those stories take hold within you. As you get older, you tend to seek out relationships and experiences that reinforce that narrative. This is called confirmation bias. These biases tend to influence how you view yourself and who you become tremendously.

Take for example the story of a young child whose older sibling has been dubbed the genius. Imagine how that younger sibling may feel knowing he may never be as smart as his older brother. He enters school, and starts to learn, and struggles because he knows he is not as smart as his brother. However, as he ages, he soon realized that he has a natural ability in something, like math or English. He reaches high school and can take advanced courses. Through this, he has effectively managed to rewrite his narrative that he had been preconditioned to. However, despite that amazing story of overcoming his predetermines vision of himself, when presented with a stressful situation, that original insecurity of not feeling smart enough may arise, causing you to feel even more overwhelmed or anxious.

Why does any of this matter? Because over years of accumulating these narratives, they have shaped you in some positive and some negative ways, wiring your brain so to speak to react and function a certain way, causing you to be inflexible when it comes to mental or emotional events. We tend to remember the negative and painful stories better than the positives. This is called negativity bias. Even though your narrative may influence your perception or reactions, it does not mean you are trapped to live them out. By paying attention to your mental awareness, you will be able to start breaking down your personal awareness, and when you are stressed, this can be an invaluable tool. That inner voice tends to get louder when you are stressed, overworked, and tired. So, by learning to pay attention to that inner voice, you can slowly start to rewire your brain.

This is one of the main goals of mindfulness. Learning to observe and pay attention to your body non-judgmentally. This takes practice, and you need to learn how to find those stories first. Here is a simple exercise for you to try as a way to identify your narrative.

Start by writing down what you feel your identity is. Simple phrases like "I am strong," or "I like to help others," or "I am really good at my job." You may also want to include things like how you were raised, experiences, family beliefs, or any other examples that shaped how you view yourself now.

Now that you have written all that down, take each one and ask yourself these questions regarding that specific phrase or experience:

- Can I change this story or am I deciding to live it?

- Does this story still apply to me?

- Whose story is this? Mine or somebody else's?

- How did this story originate?

- Am I unhappy because of this story

Being aware of your personal narrative contributes to mindfulness because you are learning what some of your inner thoughts are, that mindless chatter that is always there. By learning what causes it, you can practice mindfulness and learn to readjust your thinking, even your story, as well as reduce some of that needless stress that can arise when those negative stories come up.

Mindfulness and Being Non-Judgmental

Before you can practice non-judgment in mindfulness, it is a good idea to understand what non-judgment means. By now you should begin to understand what mindfulness means, it is the ability to be aware. Awareness on its own does not have judgment. Judgment is a thought process that can come through the awareness. This is not the kind of judgment that produces prejudices or judging someone to be inferior to you. It is the judgment of making decisions, taking making choices and putting them in the proper place. Example: When you feel that stress or depression is starting to affect you, it is important to be aware of the signs of them, then make the judgment to begin helping yourself in some way.

Non-judgment in mindfulness is used if the brain is left to its own devices, it will judge things automatically as right or wrong, fair or unfair, good or bad, important or unimportant, etc. The brain does this so fast that experiences are automatically processed as one or the other before you can take stock of it all. Mindfulness stops all this, and focuses on being aware of when these judgments are taking place, and then using that to take a brand new viewpoint.

The hard part of all of this is learning to be aware of when your brain has started to automatically judge something or a situation. If we are aware, we can take a pause and reflect on it. By doing this you will be able to take that new point of view, and then enter the non-judgmental decision-making process which mindfulness teaches.

<u>Mindfulness and Greed</u>

Greed is an innate feeling we all experience. The mind always is looking for something more. This can range anywhere from doing something new to gaining something that may bring pleasure. However, these moments of happiness last only a moment, and then what happens? We start to want more, possibly the same things or something else.

Greed is considered to be one of three unwholesome states of mind which are aversion, delusion, and greed. The defilements of the mind are a common teaching in meditation. If you have greedy thoughts, it will help them to grow, and this will start a cycle of never-ending actions which can eventually cause pain to others and yourself. Ending this cycle can be extremely hard because we live in a society that likes us to look to outside sources for happiness.

So how do we overcome wants and desires which feed into the natural tendency of the mind to be greedy? Here is an exercise you can try that will help you refocus your mind away from those desires.

- Imagine something that you want, really, really, want. Imagine yourself having that item. How does it feel to have it?

- Now let it go. Taking a deep breath, and using mindfulness, see the object for what it is, but without needing to be possessed.

- Think of what you already have. Appreciate it. How does it feel?

- Now that you have let go of the object to be obtained, how do you feel knowing that you have enough right now?

Greed is encouraged in our world because we have been conditioned to believe that more is always better. By practicing mindfulness, you can train yourself to have these thoughts, and be content with what you have right now.

- How to simplify your thoughts and desires

- What is the best possible amount: Find the middle ground. By trial and error, you will discover what your optimal amount is, or what satisfies you.

- Wants versus needs: Society bombards us daily with things we need to buy, consume, and accumulate, and this all feeds into our greed. The simplest way to not fall for marketing scams is to take stock of what you have and ask yourself "Do I NEED this, or do I WANT this." Only then will you be able to stop the greed cycle.

Avoid the trap of self-fulfilling prophecies.

What exactly is a self-fulfilling prophecy? To be able to practice this in mindfulness, you must know what this means. Basically, a self-fulfilling prophecy is when any positive or negative expectation of a circumstance, event or a person, that can affect your behavior which will cause you to act in a way that makes those expectations come true. A good example of this would be when you first meet someone, if you have a negative expectation of that person that you will not like something about them or the person as a whole, when you meet this person you will act in such a way that will cause the other person to do exactly what you thought, something to make you dislike them.

This cycle of almost self-destruction can wreak havoc when it comes to people with social anxieties, low self-esteem, and when it comes to career advancement. This self-fulfillment will eventually do exactly as you fear because your behaviors based on your negative or fearful thoughts, will show through to others and then they reciprocate those same manners.

So how can you stop this horrible trap? Mindfulness. Practicing a simple self-affirmation exercise daily can help you to overcome your tendencies to set yourself up for failure.

Mindfulness and feeling Joy for Others

A lot of people are scared to show genuine empathy for others because it means they may open themselves up to the possibility of becoming everyone else's pain and suffering. Empathy can be viewed as a stressor because dealing with everyone else's problems can cause exhaustion, and burn out.

However, in mindfulness, you can instead increase your ability to feel other people's joys, instead of building a wall against their stress. There can be great benefits to this, and it is called positive empathy, instead of the empathy that eventually causes you to want to hide from people. Studies have shown that when you have empathy for other people's pain, your brain will emulate pain of its own. The same is true of positive empathy, and when you have happiness over someone else's happiness, the brain will resonate with this as well. When you have these positive experiences, it has been shown to give more satisfaction, happiness, and peace of mind. It can also help you to gain support, greater trust, and satisfaction in close relationships.

Positive empathy, or feeling joy for others, does more than make you feel good, it can also help you to want to help others to thrive, and thus you have a stronger will to act on those feelings. Noticing joy can be easier than you think. When you think of joy, it usually presents itself as that giant smile, delight, cheers, and hugs. However, joy can be a lot smaller than that and can be found all around you. You can find joy in a delicious meal, a favorite song that comes on the radio, and the joy of hearing laughter. And these are just a few of the possible smaller joys you can find everywhere. As you practice mindfulness and awareness, the opportunities to see the joy in ordinary moments will gradually increase.

Mindfulness and liberation from suffering

Suffering and happiness cannot exist without each other. You cannot learn to be compassionate if you have never experienced suffering. However, suffering can become toxic when it is not cared for properly. You harden your heart and become overwhelmed. This then makes it impossible for you to experience compassion.

Mindfulness holds that pain is not the enemy, nor does it want to get rid of that pain. It seeks instead to help you better understand yourself and why you are in pain. By practicing mindfulness, you can start to understand what your causes of pain and suffering are, and then you will be able to liberate yourself from them.

Compassion can only arise when you mindfully take a look at your suffering and respond to it with care. As you practice mindfulness more and more, you will soon begin to discover which gestures of kindness and joy will help to open up your heart. Everyone is different in what appeals to their compassion. Once you have identified some triggers that help you, you will soon learn that even the smallest gesture of compassion will open you up to greater happiness and help to curb your suffering.

Chapter 4: Putting Mindfulness Meditation Into Practice

Well, we have made it to the final chapter, where you can see what some of the meditations practiced in mindfulness look like. These meditations are simple and can be practiced as often as you require them to remain in a Beginner's Mindset.

Mindful Breathing

What to do:

- Find a comfortable place to sit or lay down, although you can stand if necessary

- Focus your attention on your breath, inhaling and exhaling.

- Close your eyes

- Take a deep inhale through your nose and hold it for a few seconds

- Exhale slowly through your mouth

- Repeat as necessary

- A variation on this can be to just focus on your breathing, instead of using the exaggerated breaths.

- Pay attention to the rise and fall of your chest and your stomach.

- Let your breaths come naturally, whether that is slow, fast, deep, or shallow.

- The point is to focus the mind inward.

- If your mind wanders, this is fine. Just try to bring it back to the present, focusing on your breathing

Mindful Eating

What to do:

- Slow down, and give your body a chance to give your brain the signals that it is full. The reason people tend to overeat is that your stomach does not send the signal it is full as quickly as the brain deciphers that you are still hungry. This is why overeating is so easy

- Recognize what your hunger signs are. Are you hungry or are you responding to an emotional want? In a mindfulness practice of eating, listen to your body. If your stomach is growling, you are hungry. All too often the brain tells us to eat when we are not truly hungry. Mindful eating will help you to learn your body's signs of hunger.

- Eat in a healthy environment. Try not to eat alone, or wander around looking for snacks, where you are more likely to overeat and binge, but set certain times and places to eat. This simple act of making a meal and sitting at the table, especially with other people, can rewire your brain to know when it is hungry or not.

- Eat healthy foods, not foods that are comforting. Choose foods that benefit you nutritionally, not emotionally. As you practice mindful eating, it will become easier to start to think of healthier foods as comforting.

- Think of where your food came from. It is easy to not think about where food comes from beyond the supermarket, but mindful eating means to consider that food, all the people who worked to create it, from a loved one who cooked it, to the people at the store who packed it, to the farmers and ranchers who grew and raised it. By slowing down and considering this, mindful eating will bring you a greater appreciation for the food you put into your mouth.

Mindful Sounds

What to do:

Have a chime, or bell nearby on a timer, where you are sitting or laying quietly. Ring it. As the bell fades, start to listen for the following:

- Sounds in the background. Mindful hearing means letting yourself focus on those sounds that are always in the background, like a fan whirring, traffic noises, crickets. As you begin to notice them, let go and try not to identify them, but instead just take pleasure in hearing.

- Sounds of melody. Music can arouse emotions which is why music is enjoyable. When you sit quietly, you will discover melodic sounds all around you. Birds, rain on the roof, a siren. When you practice mindfulness, try to find the emotional response to each of these sounds.

- Sudden sounds. When a sudden sound interrupts us, it can shock us back into awareness. These shocking noises can wake you up and back into the present when you have been lulled into normal thought patterns.

As the ending bell fades, let that sound stay with you a moment. Then allow it to help you transition back to your day. Sounds are around you at all times, mindfulness and awareness teach to be open to them, and this one more way to appreciate the world around you.

Mindfulness of Emotion

When unpleasant emotions start to creep in, this exercise can help you to stop, refocus, and understand your current emotions.

Requires about 10 minutes, or longer

What to do:

- When you start to feel an unpleasant emotion, stop, sit, take a deep breath, and then focus on the shame, guilt, anxiety, frustration, fear, or anger that is bothering you. Do not stop it. Just sit with it in an attitude of mindful openness and acceptance.

- Pinpoint the Emotion; there could be several happening at the same time, scan your body for the strongest one at that moment.

- Acknowledge the emotion is there. Say what it is you are feeling at the moment out loud.

- Take several more deep breaths, then accept what it is. You do not need to deny these emotions have risen, instead accept it for what it is, be in the present, and say to yourself "I accept that I feel very angry right now.".

- Open and embrace the emotion. Through acceptance, you can embrace the feeling in your awareness, which can be soothing and help you move on from the emotion faster. In this space, you learn that you are not your anger, fear, or embarrassment. You are bigger than that.

- Realize that all Emotions are not permanent. They come, they stay for a while, and then they go away. Your job in mindfulness is to simply be aware

that they are there, and accept you are
feeling them.

- Do not consider yourself in a negative
  light because you are experiencing these
  emotions. Mindfulness can help you to
  see these emotions as a mental event
  that is passing through, just like waves
  in the ocean coming in and receding on
  a beach

- Figure out where emotion came from
  and then respond to it. Once you have
  calmed down from this emotion, look
  into yourself and try to investigate what
  may have brought on the emotion. Once
  you have identified the cause, you can
  reflect on it, embrace them, realize that
  it is what it is, and move on about your
  day.

- Be open to the outcomes of your emotions. Denying them will only elevate them within you, and it will not give you the opportunity to examine them to see what your triggers are, and through that, you can program your brain to react differently the next time a similar situation arises.

Here is a quick version of the emotional acceptance exercise, one you write down and keep in your pocket if you need to:

Emotional Acceptance in 4 easy steps:

- Observe: Become aware of the feelings in your body

- Breathe: Take several deep breaths. Breathe in and out

- Expand: Allow room for these emotions, create a space for them

- Allow: Allow the emotions be there, do not shove them aside.

<u>Mindfulness and Thoughts</u>

One of the most common exercises taught for Mindfulness of Thoughts is called "Leaves in a Stream."

Takes about 10 minutes

- Imagine you are sitting by a stream, with the water in front of you

- Listen for any sounds from the water

- Look for any trees around the stream

- Look at the stream, are there any leaves from these trees floating in it

- Now, as a thought enters your mind, acknowledge it, then put it onto one of those leaves floating in the stream

- Watch the stream float away

- Repeat this with every thought you have during the duration of the exercise

- Once you acknowledge your thoughts, you do not need to keep them. You do not need to feel attached to these thoughts

- Only acknowledge, then let it float away on a leaf

- By allowing these thoughts to go away, it lessens the hold on you these thoughts have and their intensity.

- By lessening them, you can clear the chatter in your mind, and be more mindful of the now, and aware of your body.

Another exercise to help you with thoughts and mindfulness is called RAIN, an acronym to help you remember how to practice mindfulness:

R: Recognize what is happening

A: Allow that experience to be there as it is

I: Investigate it with kindness

N: Natural awareness comes from not identifying with the current experience

Recognize: This means that you are acknowledging the thoughts and feelings within you. The first step to cleansing yourself of negative thoughts is to just recognize that they are there. Common negative feelings include fear, unworthiness, shame, anxiety, depression, and a critical inner voice. Everyone has a different response to each of these emotions, some stay very busy to avoid these feelings or prove to themselves they are valuable, others freeze because they are scared of failure. Still, others may develop addictive behaviors like alcohol, drugs, or overeating as a way to face their shame or fear. Whichever of these people you are more like, remember that it is unhealthy, and recognizing your emotions and thoughts can help you to slowly cleanse yourself of them.

Allowing: This means that your emotions, feelings, sensations, and thoughts are all recognized as just being there. People react to unpleasant experiences in three different ways, numbing yourself to the feeling, stacking up the judgment, or placing your attention somewhere else. None of these corrects the current experience, and they do not help your brain to react differently the next time something similar occurs. By allowing those thoughts or feelings to be there, you are honestly accepting and acknowledging the presence of them.

Investigate: This means that you are activating your curiosity, the yearning to want to find the truth, which can then direct your focus to your present moment. By pausing for a moment and asking yourself what is happening to me, you can begin to investigate these feelings. Unless you examine these feelings and thoughts and bring them out to be looked at further, these thoughts or feeling will always control how you react when a similar situation happens again

Natural loving awareness: This means that when identification of the smaller things is found, you can loosen yourself. The practice of non-identification helps us to become not stuck with any of your emotions, sensations, or stories. You can begin to live with openness and express your awareness. Loving awareness is a liberating feeling, the ability to function in a natural state of awareness. As you continue to practice mindfulness, you will begin to notice a change in how you see things, how you react to them, and how you can learn from these experiences the next time they arise.

Throughout your life, you have been conditioned to live within certain boundaries, certain expectations, certain uncertainties. It is the nature of the world around us with all of the craziness of school, work, relationships, and relaxations. The world would have you believe that you must own certain things to be happy, and how much of it you should have. Technology has become a daily way of life, and we find ourselves becoming more and more addicted to it. This can all play into the innate feelings of greed as well as the feelings of self-worth. You have been conditioned to believe that you are worth more in other's eyes if you have a college degree, the newest cars, the newest phones, the best TV streaming abilities, and of course, how much money you make. Society expects you to put on a showy display, and through that, you have learned to find your feelings of fulfillment, self-worth, completeness, aliveness, intelligence, and love.

As we have discussed in this book, through the practice of Beginner's Mindset, practicing mindfulness, awareness, and following the exercises in this book, you can begin the process of slowly cleansing yourself of these preconditioned mindsets. Just because your environment says one thing, you have the power within you to change how you view it. You can harness the power of your brain and learn to be aware of your thoughts, your feelings, and the feelings and thoughts of those around you. Mindfulness will help you to understand all of these things, and allow you to live in the moment, instead of the future, or the past, dwelling on possible outcomes that do not pertain to you in the now. Every day presents its own stresses and anxieties, so live each day to its fullest, never worrying about yesterday's problems or tomorrows possibilities. Mindfulness and awareness will help you to stay present and focus on the most important things: you, what you are feeling now, what you are doing now, how you fix things now, and how you learn to prevent them now.

Final Thoughts

Thank you for making it to the end of this book. We hope *Mindfulness for Beginners: Make the Most Out of Your Life* was informative and able to provide you with all of the tools you need to achieve your goals on your path to mindfulness. Now you should be well on your way to starting a life full of awareness and being in the moment. We hope that after reading this book, even the most novice in beginner's mindset should be able to walk away and feel confident about starting to practice the way to mindfulness

Mindfulness and Awareness hold keys to inner peace, and with that peace, you can become a better person. You learned how to pause, put your mind at that moment and focus on where you are, what you are doing, and how it is affecting you. Mindfulness can help refocus you on many aspects of your life, family, work, relationships, and more. It can help reduce stress, and with daily practice, it can even eliminate it.

In this book you also learned several techniques and exercises to practice at home and throughout your day such as mindfulness breathing, eating, emotions, thoughts, and awareness. The exercises will help you to find your way to a Beginner's Mindset.

The next step is to go out there and start your Beginner's Mindset, and embark on living a healthier you.

Finally, if you found this book useful in any way, a review on Amazon is always appreciated!

The following eBook is reproduced below with the goal of providing information that is as accurate and reliable as possible. Regardless, purchasing this eBook can be seen as consent to the fact that both the publisher and the author of this book are in no way experts on the topics discussed within and that any recommendations or suggestions that are made herein are for entertainment purposes only. Professionals should be consulted as needed prior to undertaking any of the action endorsed herein.

This declaration is deemed fair and valid by both the American Bar Association and the

The information in the following pages is broadly considered to be a truthful and accurate account of facts, and as such any inattention, use or misuse of the information in question by the reader will render any resulting actions solely under their purview. There are no scenarios in which the publisher or the original author of this work can be in any fashion deemed liable for any hardship or damages that may befall them after undertaking information described herein.

Additionally, the information in the following pages is intended only for informational purposes and should thus be thought of as universal. As befitting its nature, it is presented without assurance regarding its prolonged validity or interim quality. Trademarks that are mentioned are done without written consent and can in no way be considered an endorsement from the trademark holder.